SAMURAI UNDRESSED

by Jacqui Carey.

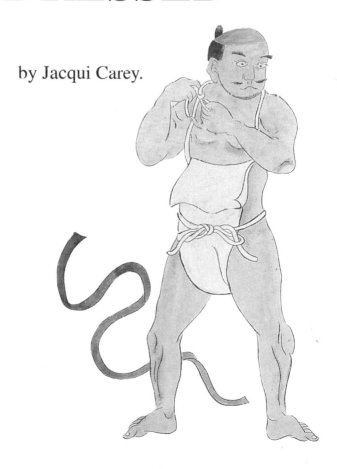

Published by Carey Company
Copyright © 1995 Jacqui Carey.

Printed in England by The Devonshire Press Ltd, Torquay.

ISBN 0 9523225 1 X

ACKNOWLEDGEMENTS

"Samurai Undressed" has come about through the overwhelming
generosity, enthusiasm and expertise of so many people.
It has been a combined effort of contributions both big and small,
each playing an important part in creating the whole.
Particular thanks goes to the following; John Anderson,
Ian Bottomley, The Braid Society, Eric Bransden,
The Chester Beatty Library, Creative Exhibitions Ltd.,
Marion Edwards, Exeter Royal Albert Memorial Museum,
Gail Forrest, Cas Holmes, Jock Hopson, Gregory Irvine,
The Japanese Embassy, Masiko Kinoshita,
Steve & Avril Smith, Noemi Speiser,
The Surrey Institute of Art & Design, Makiko Tada.

Dedicated to my family,
for they have given the most.

Introduction.

A suit of Samurai armour is a visually stunning work of art.
Close examination reveals a wealth of intriguing detail and
a beauty so particular to Japanese craftsmanship.
A technique that has played an important part in armour construction,
is Kumihimo, the art of Japanese braidmaking.
The silk braids not only provided the necessary strength and flexibility
needed to connect the lamellar armour, but also added to the
aesthetic beauty of the suit.

"Samurai Undressed" attempts to reveal some of the hidden
depths of Samurai armour and its unique
relationship with Kumihimo.

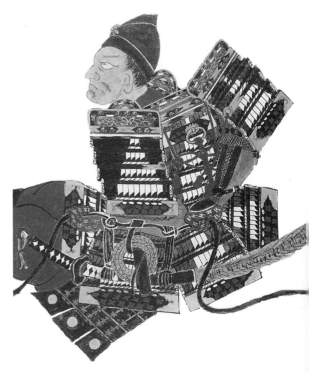

EARLY HISTORY

JOMON

The exact origins of Kumihimo are difficult to trace. This is mainly due to the hot, humid climate of Japan, which makes things decompose very quickly.
Little is left of the early braids as textiles are particularly susceptible to this process.
The earliest evidence of cords can be found from the earthenware pots of the Jomon period[1].

Cords were pressed into wet clay to create the decorative patterns found on these vessels.
This practise was so widespread that the era was named Jomon, *(Cord patterned).*Although there are a wide variety of markings on the pots, it is hard to establish the structure of the braids used.

---

[1] *Jomon period runs up to 8AD.*
(N.B. Dates of eras vary. The dates used here are from
"Nihonshi no Yoryo" by Suwa Tokutaro, Obunsha, Tokyo, 1957.)

HANIWA

Since early times, people have migrated from China and Korea to Japan.

They brought with them new ideas and influences from the mainland.

From this source came the introduction of dolmen burials. The large burial mounds, called Kofun, provide the first evidence of the early armour.

The earliest style of armour excavated from these mounds is known as Tanko.

It was constructed from large iron plates held together with leather thongs.

This style was gradually superseded when lamellar armour, called Keiko, was introduced.

Lamellar armour is made from overlapping rectangular scales of metal or leather, which are laced together in a row. Each row is then overlapped and laced together to form a flexible yet protective armour.

It is an ancient technique that originates in the Middle East.

Though only a certain number of actual suits of armour have been excavated, the combination of the Tanko and Keiko styles and their subsequent development can be seen from the Haniwa Figures.

These fired clay figures, found around the graves of the Yamato[2] elite, also depict detail of cords and ties used in the armour. Many of these were probably made from leather or cloth rather than woven braids. However, two types of woven braid have been identified[3] on excavated armour.

---

[2] *The Yamato people formed the first Japanese state in around 300AD, consisting of provinces ruled by a central court.*

[3] *A 1819 copy of "Mano-Ke Den Kojitsu Itokumi Tetsuke" (The Proprietary Braiding Techniques of the Mano family).*

SHOSOIN

As the introduced religion of Buddhism gathered strength, the practise of building Kofun declined and the Japanese way of life was increasingly influenced by Chinese culture.

An Imperial court was established in Nara, the first true capital of Japan.

It was here that the Shosoin storehouse was built for the Todai-ji Temple, the largest temple in the city.

In 756, Empress Komyo began donating items to the temple, mainly things belonging to her deceased husband, Emperor Shomu.

Other items held at the Shosoin repository came from the monastery at Todai-ji; many of these can also be dated to the 8th century.

Although 90 Keiko and 10 Tanko suits of armour were originally stored here too, they were borrowed to arm imperial troops and were never returned.

Only a few fragments remain of a Keiko laced in purple doeskin.

However, many of the other items, adorned with braids, have survived to provide the best source of information on early woven braids.

Uses for these braids were varied and included: belts; ties for bags; costume decoration and ornamental hems; hanging cords for knives and ornaments ; decorative attachments on mirrors, musical instruments and sports items; ties for scrolls and banners.

Although the braids are made from several different structures, square braids are the most predominant. Their construction is supportive of the theory that they were made using loop manipulation technique *(see Kute-uchi page 65).*

STYLES OF ARMOUR

O-YOROI

It is uncertain how many of the early braids were foreign imports or of Japanese origin. But, during the early Heian[1] period, the Japanese were distancing themselves from China, and were adapting their own distinct style and character.

This was combined with the development of a refined culture within the aristocracy. These two factors effected all forms of art including braidmaking.

The armour belonging to the military elite became more elaborate as befitting their status and fashionable tastes.

The Keiko was developed into what is known as the O-Yoroi. *(Great Armour)* This style of armour was adapted for the manner of warfare being used, that of mounted archery.

Battles tended to be internal disputes between the imperial forces and those of the aristocratic landowners, with the Samurai *(one who serves)* emerging as loyal warriors allied to one particular family.

Battles often took the form of charges from the horse riding Samurai who shouted out their pedigree and achievements before firing their arrows at the enemy, then wheeling back to the home lines.

With each Samurai intent on personal glory, there was little or no tactical strategy involved.

By the 12th century, braiding had developed further. Artistically, braiding reached its zenith with the complex braids used at court and in the temples, *(see plate 4)*.

In the utilitarian world of armour lacing, the 2 or 4 ridge flat braid had given way to a flat 8-ridge braid, *(see plate 38)*. Although it was more time consuming to make, it was narrower and more supple.

When these braids were combined with narrower scales that were moulded in an outwards curve, the armour took on a stronger and less clumsy appearance.

---

[1] *Early Heian period 794-898 AD, Late Heian period 898-1185 AD.*
Named after the new capital at Heian-Kyo ("Capital of peace and tranquillity")
on the site of modern Kyoto.

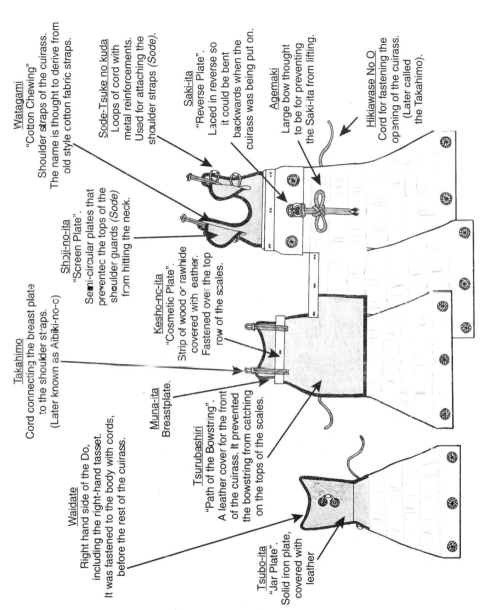

Watagami "Cotton Chewing". Shoulder straps of the cuirass. The name is thought to derive from old style cotton fabric straps.

Sode-Tsuke no kuda Loops of cord with metal reinforcements. Used for attaching the shoulder straps (*Sode*).

Saki-ita "Reverse Plate". Laced in reverse so it could be bent backwards when the cuirass was being put on.

Agemaki Large bow thought to be for preventing the Saki-ita from lifting.

Hikiawase No O Cord for fastening the opening of the cuirass. (Later called the Takahimo).

Shoji-no-ita "Screen Plate". Semi-circular plates that prevented the tops of the shoulder guards (*Sode*) from hitting the neck.

Takahimo Cord connecting the breast plate to the shoulder straps. (Later known as Aibiki-no-o)

Kesho-no-ita "Cosmetic Plate". Strip of wood or rawhide covered with leather. Fastened over the top row of the scales.

Muna-ita Breastplate.

Waidate Right hand side of the Do, including the right-hand tasset. It was fastened to the body with cords, before the rest of the cuirass.

Tsurubashiri "Path of the Bowstring". A leather cover for the front of the cuirass. It prevented the bowstring from catching on the tops of the scales.

Tsubo-ita "Jar Plate". Solid iron plate, covered with leather

DIAGRAM 1: The Do (*cuirass*) of a O-Yoroi resembles a box-like structure made in two parts. The main section covered the front, left and back sides of the wearer. The right hand side was a separate section and was fitted independently.

DO-MARU

The Gempei war of the late 12th century resulted in a shift of power to the town of Kamakura. It was the start of a long era of military ruling in spite of the Emperor still holding court at Kyoto.

Although this affected the politics of Japan, it had little effect on the manner of fighting.

This was to change in 1274 when Kublai Khan's Mongolian troops invaded Japan. The ritualistic challenges of the Samurai warriors were totally useless against the well disciplined army. The Japanese only survived because the foreign fleet was destroyed by storms.

When the Mongols returned with more troops in 1281, the Japanese were better prepared. But once again it was nature that destroyed the fleet with a tornado. Another factor to change the style of warfare was the long internal struggle for power known as the Nambokucho[2] War .

Much of this was fought on difficult terrain, bringing about an increase in hand to hand fighting. The emphasis changed from mounted archery to sword fighting on foot.

This had its effect on the sort of protection required by the warriors. Ideas from the O-Yoroi were combined with the Haramaki *(belly wrapping)* This was a mode of armour worn by the common foot soldiers.

These retainers had previously served the Samurai warriors but had done little of the actual fighting. Their armour was of the same lamellar construction, but formed long rows that reached all the way round the torso. These were held in place with straps over the shoulders.

Protection for the shoulders came in the form of small plates called 'Gyoyo' *(apricot leaves)*. The tassets *(kusazuri)* hanging from the waist were divided into 7 or 8 sections, making it easier for walking.

Do-Maru *(Body round)* became the style favoured by the Samurai due to its practical nature.

---

2 *period of Northern and Southern Courts 1336-1392 AD.*

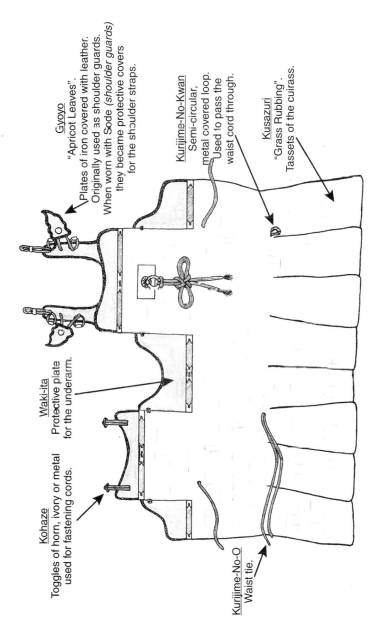

Gyoyo
"Apricot Leaves".
Plates of iron covered with leather.
Originally used as shoulder guards.
When worn with Sode (*shoulder guards*)
they became protective covers
for the shoulder straps.

Kurijime-No-Kwan
Semi-circular,
metal covered loop.
Used to pass the
waist cord through.

Kusazuri
"Grass Rubbing".
Tassets of the cuirass.

Waki-ita
Protective plate
for the underarm.

Kohaze
Toggles of horn, ivory or metal
used for fastening cords.

Kurijime-No-O
Waist tie.

DIAGRAM 2: The Do of the Do-Maru was made in one piece, wrapping round the
body with the join under the right arm. This style of armour was
intended for the swordsman on foot.

TOSEI GUSOKU

The Muromachi[3] period settled down after the Nambokucho war, but the struggle for power did not cease.

Rivalry between two opposing families escalated into the Onin war in 1467, which destroyed much of Kyoto. It also saw the beginning of what is known as the Sengoku *(Age of War 1482-1558 AD)*.

During this period, numerous power struggles took place resulting in a constant demand for arms and armour. This was augmented by the deployment of large armies of common soldiers, all of whom needed equipping.

Various styles and innovations were tried out in an attempt to produce practical solutions to the demand. This saw the rise of Tosei Gusoku *(Modern armour)*.

The style took on many forms, with the general trend towards simpler, sturdier suits. Sugake lacing *(see page 62)* was one of the developments that helped to increase the metal plate areas. This cut down on the labour-intensive braidwork and improved the cleanliness of the suits.

In the early 1540's, Portuguese seafarers introduced the Japanese to guns.

The production and use of these firearms quickly spread and, with it, an increase in the popularity of solid metal plate cuirasses.

Other foreign influences also managed to find their way into the 'Modern Armours', such as Western shaped helmets and the use of foreign fabrics.

---

[3] *Muromachi period 1333-1573 AD.*
Named after a district of Kyoto where the ruling Asikagu Shoguns had their head quarters.

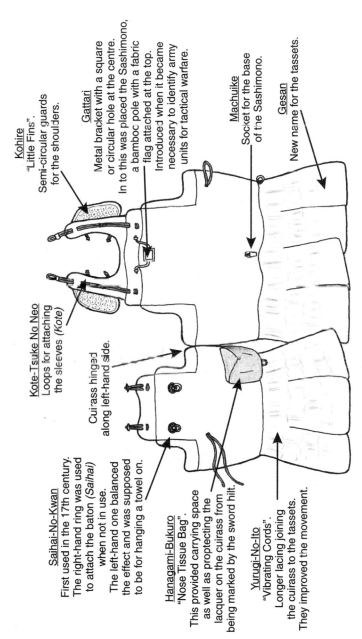

Kohire
"Little Fins".
Semi-circular guards
for the shoulders.

Gattari
Metal bracket with a square
or circular hole at the centre.
In to this was placed the Sashimono,
a bamboc pole with a fabric
flag attached at the top.
Introduced when it became
necessary to identify army
units for tactical warfare.

Machuike
Socket for the base
of the Sashimono.

Gesan
New name for the tassets.

Kote-Tsuke No Neo
Loops for attaching
the sleeves (*Kote*)

Cuirass hinged
along left-hand side.

Saihai-No-Kwan
First used in the 17th century.
The right-hand ring was used
to attach the baton (*Saihai*)
when not in use.
The left-hand one balanced
the effect and was supposed
to be for hanging a towel on.

Hanagami-Bukuro
"Nose Tissue Bag".
This provided carrying space
as well as proptecting the
lacquer on the cuirass from
being marked by the sword hilt.

Yurugi-No-Ito
"Vibrating Cords".
Longer lacing joining
the cuirass to the tassets.
They improved the movement.

DIAGRAM 3: The Cuirass of a Tosei Gusoku, armour of a utilitarian nature
benefiting from the application of more solid plates

PLATE 1: Tosei-Gusoku *(Modern armour)* made for a low ranking warrior.
The Mon *(family crest)* on the front of the Do *(Cuirass)* is of a water plantain plant.
Courtesy of Surrey Institute of Art & Design

PLATE 2: Drawing of a common foot soldier, armed with a gun. The circular items around his neck are his rations, balls of rice wrapped in material.

Courtesy of the Anderson Collection.

THE EDO PERIOD.

The unification of Japan was bought about under the direction of three men :
Oda Nobunaga, Toyotomi Hideyoshi and Tokugawa Ieyasu. But it wasn't until Icyasu's leadership that peace was finally restored to Japan.

The capital was moved to Edo and a rigid class structure was established, with the Samurai holding an elite status.

The Edo period[4] saw Japan cutting its links with the outside world and tightening its internal control. It was the start of an era of peace.

The Samurai became increasingly bureaucratic, and this was to affect the role of their armour.

By the 1700's, there was a trend towards armour that reflected the grandeur of the past, with old styles such as the O-Yoroi and Do-maru becoming fashionable once more.

The production of these armours had never really ceased as there had always been a demand for unusual, personalised suits.

Now, however, the practicalities of the armour were disregarded in favour of decorative appeal. Certain features from different styles were copied without regard to their purpose, resulting in unusual and ineffective armour.

Throughout history, decorative armour had not been in general use but had had its place as ceremonial dress or as votive offerings to religious shrines and temples.

A small revival for more utilitarian armour occurred in the early 1800's, but, without the need for protective armour, the emphasise still tended towards outward appearances rather than function.

---

4 *Edo period 1603-1868 AD.*
Named after the capital, Edo, on the site of modern Tokyo.

PLATE 3: A Boy's Festive Suit in the O-Yoroi style,
intended for the mounted archer.
Courtesy of J.Hopson.

PLATE 4: Reproduction of the braid known as Saidaiji, named after the temple in which it was found. This originally dates from the 13th century and was used as a drawstring for a pouch containing a Buddhist scroll.

Courtesy of Rodrick Owen.

PLATE 5 : A fine half face mask(*Mempo*)with detachable nose. It is signed "Myochin Osumi No Kami Munesuke" a member of a family of famous armour makers. The feature lines are of gold and silver lacquer.

Courtesy of the Anderson Collection.

PLATE 6 : A Samurai helmet *(Kabuto).*
Courtesy of Exeter Royal Albert Memorial Museum.

SINGLE PIECES

It is worth noting that armour came in a whole manner of different styles.
Although coordinated suits were desired, if the need arose, various parts of different
suits would be worn together as a set .
It was not uncommon for old suits to be re-laced or refashioned into new styles
adding to the unique quality of each suit of armour.

HELMET

The Helmet *(Kabuto)* came in a wide variety of designs. Some were formed in
unusual designs or were worn with extravagant crests.
As with other pieces of high quality armour, there was a great attention to detail.
The picture below shows the interior of the helmet bowl, revealing the fabric lining
known as Ukebari. These were introduced during the Nambokucho war. They were
usually made in one piece and stitched in a spiral to gather them into shape.
Sometimes the lining had a small slit at the back. This was to reveal the
manufacturers signature on the metal interior.

PLATE 7 : Interior of a helmet bowl, showing the fabric lining *(Ukebari)*.

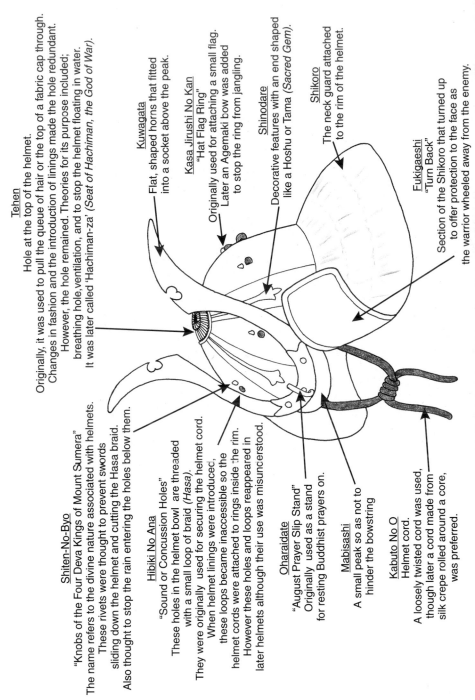

Tehen
Hole at the top of the helmet.
Originally, it was used to pull the queue of hair or the top of a fabric cap through.
Changes in fashion and the introduction of linings made the hole redundant.
However, the hole remained. Theories for its purpose included;
breathing hole, ventilation, and to stop the helmet floating in water.
It was later called 'Hachiman-za' *(Seat of Hachiman, the God of War)*.

Kuwagata
Flat, shaped horns that fitted
into a socket above the peak.

Kasa Jirushi No Kan
"Hat Flag Ring"
Originally used for attaching a small flag.
Later an Agemaki bow was added
to stop the ring from jangling.

Shinodare
Decorative features with an end shaped
like a Hoshu or Tama *(Sacred Gem)*.

Shikoro
The neck guard attached
to the rim of the helmet.

Fukigaeshi
"Turn Back"
Section of the Shikoro that turned up
to offer protection to the face as
the warrior wheeled away from the enemy.

Shiten-No-Byo
"Knobs of the Four Deva Kings of Mount Sumera"
The name refers to the divine nature associated with helmets.
These rivets were thought to prevent swords
sliding down the helmet and cutting the Hasa braid.
Also thought to stop the rain entering the holes below them.

Hibiki No Ana
"Sound or Concussion Holes"
These holes in the helmet bowl are threaded
with a small loop of braid *(Hasa)*.
They were originally used for securing the helmet cord.
When helmet linings were introduced,
these loops became inaccessible so the
helmet cords were attached to rings inside the rim.
However these holes and loops reappeared in
later helmets although their use was misunderstood.

Oharaidate
"August Prayer Slip Stand"
Originally used as a stand
for resting Buddhist prayers on.

Mabisashi
A small peak so as not to
hinder the bowstring

Kabuto No O
Helmet cord.
A loosely twisted cord was used,
though later a cord made from
silk crepe rolled around a core,
was preferred.

DIAGRAM 4 : The Helmet *(Kabuto).*

CUIRASS

The main body of the armour was called the Do. *(See plate 27 and diagrams 1-3)*
In later years, some suits had detachable tassets *(Gesan).* These were removed
whilst marching. Other tassets had ties so that they could be gathered up.

PLATE 8 : Detachable Tassets*(Gesan)* attached to a leather waist band so that
   they could be removed whilst marching. These ones also have a
   pocket hidden behind the central tasset.

Courtesy of Exeter Royal Albert Memorial Museum.

FACE MASK

Armour for the face *(Men gu)* came in various styles. Early ones, known as Happuri, covered just the forehead and cheeks. Later styles tended towards protection for the lower face. *(See plate 5).* The interior of the mask was usually lacquered red. This was to give the face an angry glow.

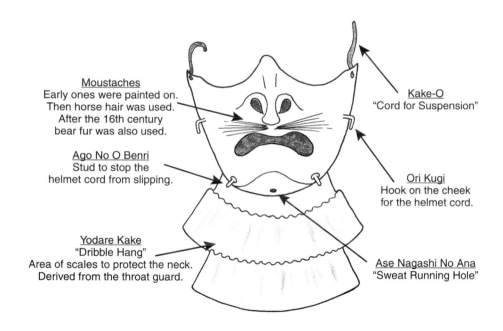

Moustaches
Early ones were painted on.
Then horse hair was used.
After the 16th century
bear fur was also used.

Kake-O
"Cord for Suspension"

Ago No O Benri
Stud to stop the
helmet cord from slipping.

Ori Kugi
Hook on the cheek
for the helmet cord.

Yodare Kake
"Dribble Hang"
Area of scales to protect the neck.
Derived from the throat guard.

Ase Nagashi No Ana
"Sweat Running Hole"

DIAGRAM 5 : Face Mask.

THROAT GUARD

The throat guard was known as Nodawa. It was originally used with just a face mask. When the face mask combined with the throat guard to form the Yodare Kake, the throat guard was no longer necessary. However, in later years the use of the Nodawa was misunderstood and they were worn together.

PLATE 9 : Throat Guard(*Nodawa*) from the Edo period, with a central,
decorative Agemaki knot.

Courtesy of the Anderson Collection.

SHOULDER GUARDS

The Shoulder guards, known as Sode, acted as shields for the mounted archers. They were attached to the warrior, leaving their hands free for fighting.

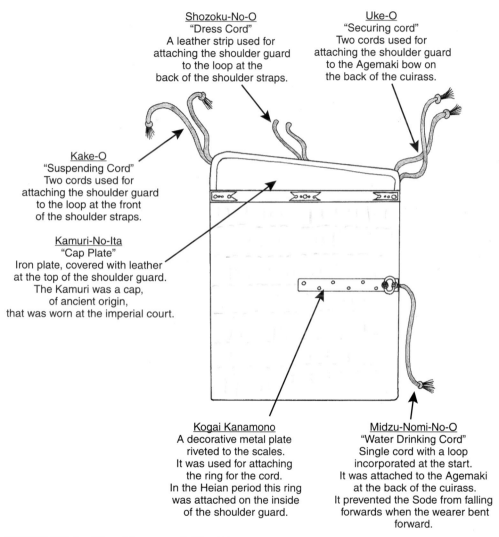

Shozoku-No-O
"Dress Cord"
A leather strip used for
attaching the shoulder guard
to the loop at the
back of the shoulder straps.

Uke-O
"Securing cord"
Two cords used for
attaching the shoulder guard
to the Agemaki bow on
the back of the cuirass.

Kake-O
"Suspending Cord"
Two cords used for
attaching the shoulder guard
to the loop at the front
of the shoulder straps.

Kamuri-No-Ita
"Cap Plate"
Iron plate, covered with leather
at the top of the shoulder guard.
The Kamuri was a cap,
of ancient origin,
that was worn at the imperial court.

Kogai Kanamono
A decorative metal plate
riveted to the scales.
It was used for attaching
the ring for the cord.
In the Heian period this ring
was attached on the inside
of the shoulder guard.

Midzu-Nomi-No-O
"Water Drinking Cord"
Single cord with a loop
incorporated at the start.
It was attached to the Agemaki
at the back of the cuirass.
It prevented the Sode from falling
forwards when the wearer bent
forward.

DIAGRAM 6 : Shoulder guard *(Sode).*

PLATE 10 : A pair of Shoulder guards *(Sode)* carefully laced and lacquered
to depict the Sun and Moon.

Courtesy of the Anderson Collection.

SLEEVES

The detachable, armoured sleeves were known as Kote. They had a material base which was then covered in chain mail and metal plates.

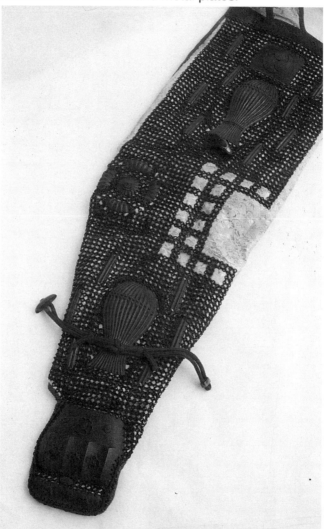

PLATE 11 : Sleeve *(Kote)* covered in mail with Gourd shaped plates *(Fukube).* Occasionally these are found with small compartments inside, for storing medicines.

Courtesy of Exeter Royal Albert Memorial Museum.

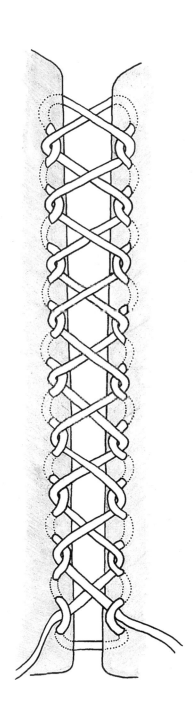

DIAGRAM 7 :

The lacing on the underside of the
sleeve was usually done with a round,
plain weave braid.
Either one or two cords were used.
Diagram shows just one way of lacing
up a sleeve with a single cord.

THIGH GUARDS :

Thigh guards *(Haidate)* took the form of an apron like garment.

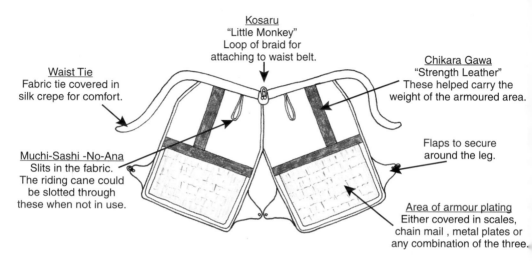

Kosaru
"Little Monkey"
Loop of braid for
attaching to waist belt.

Chikara Gawa
"Strength Leather"
These helped carry the
weight of the armoured area.

Waist Tie
Fabric tie covered in
silk crepe for comfort.

Muchi-Sashi -No-Ana
Slits in the fabric.
The riding cane could
be slotted through
these when not in use.

Flaps to secure
around the leg.

Area of armour plating
Either covered in scales,
chain mail , metal plates or
any combination of the three.

DIAGRAM 8: Thigh guards *(Haidate).*

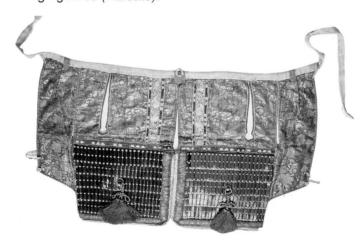

PLATE 12 : Thigh Guards made from silk brocade and lacquered scales.

Courtesy of Exeter Royal Albert Memorial Museum.

— 30 —

SHIN GUARDS

High riding boots were normally worn with the early armours. Armoured Shin guards *(Suneate)* were worn when the warriors started wearing shoes.

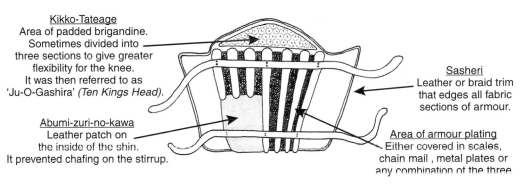

Kikko-Tateage
Area of padded brigandine.
Sometimes divided into
three sections to give greater
flexibility for the knee.
It was then referred to as
'Ju-O-Gashira' *(Ten Kings Head).*

Abumi-zuri-no-kawa
Leather patch on
the inside of the shin.
It prevented chafing on the stirrup.

Sasheri
Leather or braid trim
that edges all fabric
sections of armour.

Area of armour plating
Either covered in scales,
chain mail , metal plates or
any combination of the three

DIAGRAM 9 : A Shin Guard *(Suneate).*

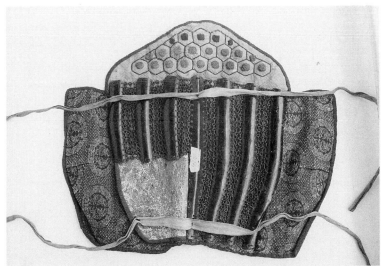

PLATE 13 : A Shin guard with splint like metal plates connected with chain-mail.
Courtesy of Exeter Royal Albert Memorial Museum.

FOOTWEAR

O-Yoroi style suits were worn with bear fur riding boots.

These became impractical when the emphases changed to fighting on foot.

The Samurai then adopted small fur shoes or the rice straw sandals *(Waraji)* , commonly worn by the lower ranks.*(See plate 2).*

'Tabi' socks which divide at the big toe, could be worn with these sandals.

The straw sandals were disposable and distances were measured in the number of pairs required for each journey.

PLATE 14 : A bear fur shoe *(Tsuranuki)* .

Courtesy of Exeter Royal Albert Memorial Museum.

UNDERCLOTHES

Undergarments for the Samurai came in as large a variety as the armour itself.
A loincloth known as a Fundoshi was one of the foundation garments worn by the
Samurai, followed by a plain shirt-like garment called a Shitagi. This was tied at the
waist with a material obi sash.

Over these undergarments was worn the Yoroi Hitatare *(Armour robe)*. It consisted
of a short kimono top with large sleeves and matching breeches known as Hakama.
They were usually made from rich brocade and were based on court costume. The
sleeves and legs both ended in a drawstring. This enabled the ends to be gathered.
The sleeve drawstring formed a loop which was placed over the gloves to stop the
sleeve riding up. The legging were drawn up so they could be tucked into the riding
boots. With the advent of armoured sleeves and shin guards , the Yoroi Hitatare
developed a closer fit, alleviating the need for drawstrings.
The armour was then worn over the Yoroi Hitatare.
The following sequence *(Plates 15-28)*
is taken from an armour book *(dated 1801)*
showing a warrior dressing in an
O-Yoroi style suit.
It illustrates the various undergarments
and pieces of armour that would
have been worn at this time.

PLATE 15 : Samurai in his loincloth *(Fundoshi).*

PLATE 16 : (top left)
>Tieing the sash around

PLATE 17 : (top right)
>Putting on the cloth hat,
>after having donned the
>armour robe, *(Yoroi Hitatare,*
>consisting of a kimono top
>and matching trousers.

PLATE 18 : (left)
>Donning material leggings
>*(Kiahan)*
>and archery gloves *(Yugake).*

Courtesy of the Anderson Collection.

PLATE 19 : (top left)
    Tightening the drawstring of the
    sleeves with a loop over the gloves.
    The bear fur boots *(Tsuranuki)*
    are already in place.

PLATE 20 : (top right)
    First the thigh guards *(Haidate)*
    are tied around the waist, then the
    right-hand side of the cuirass
    (Waidate) is attached around
    the waist and shoulder.
    The armoured sleeves *(Kote)*
    are attached across the back
    of the neck and finally the
    throat guard *(Nodawa)*
    is fitted around the neck.

PLATE 21: (right)
    Donning the cuirass *(Do)*
    with the shoulder guards *(Sode)*
    and shoulder strap guards
    (Sendan and Kyubi) already attached.
    Tieing the over belt *(Uwa-obi)*
    around the waist.

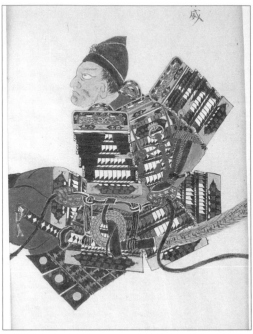

PLATE 22 : (top left)
　　　Tieing on the small sword
　　　(Koshi-gatana).
PLATE 23 : (top right)
　　　Tieing the long sword
　　　(Tachi) around the waist.
PLATE 24 : (right)
　　　 Addition of the
　　　helmet *(Kabuto)* and
　　　cheek guards *(Happuri)*
　　　and tightening the cords
　　　around the wrists.

Courtesy of the Anderson Collection.

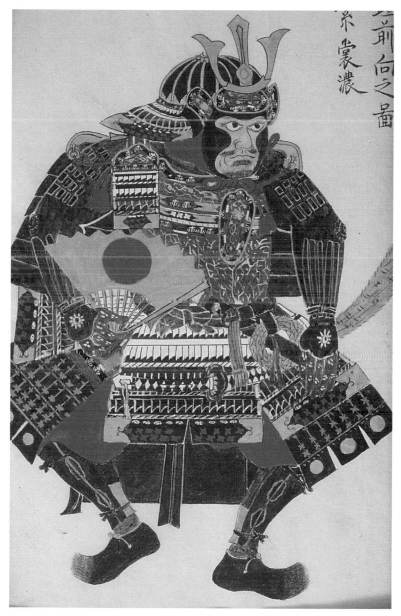

PLATE 25 : Fully dressed Samurai complete with battle fan

Courtesy of the Anderson Collection.

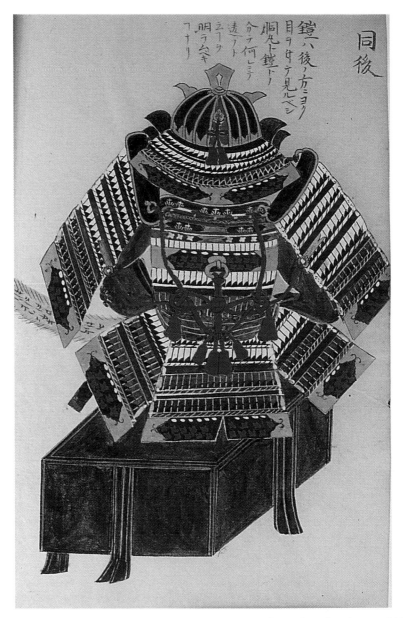

PLATE 26 : The same Samurai seen from the back. Showing the Agemaki bow
with Shoulder guard *(Sode)* cords attached.

Courtesy of the Anderson Collection.

— 38 —

PLATE 27 : Cuirass *(Do)* of Tosei-Gusoku *(Modern Armour)* style.
Courtesy of Exeter Royal Albert Memorial Museum.

PLATE 28 : Painting of common soldiers. The one on horseback, with the ladle, is a water-taster. Horse is wearing armour, an Edo adaption, with large cords as decorative and functional features.

Courtesy of the Anderson Collection.

— 40 —

ASSOCIATED PIECES

Kumihimo braids had a whole range of uses throughout all walks of life; from the mundane tie of an Inro[1], to the magnificent binding on a religious scroll.

In the military class, braids were not just applied to armour. Kumihimo ties were also utilised on horns, batons, swords and other items.

SWORDS

Swords replaced the bow and arrow as the Samurai's main weapon. They became skillfully made and highly prized.

Braids used on these swords were both functional and decorative, an attribute so typical of Japanese work.

Hilt braids were more often plain than patterned. They were bound around the hilt in a decorative twist that created diamond shaped 'windows'. These revealed the Same[2] and metal work underneath. The texture of the binding was designed to improve the grip.

The Sageo *(cord for attaching the scabbard to a belt)* was generally a more flamboyant design, often reflecting the quality of the sword and the status of its owner.

A popular Sageo was a double cloth braid called 'Kikko'. (Tortoise) This was favoured as the tortoise is associated with a long life. The design could be worked in a variety of styles and complexities. *(See plate 36).*

BOY'S FESTIVAL SUITS

Every year, miniature suits of armour are displayed as part of the Boy's Festival celebrations. *(See plate 3).*

This festival *(Tango no Sekku)* always takes place on 5th May. The girls have their own 'Dolls' festival on 3rd March.

---

[1] *Inro is the name given to the small lacquered pouch worn hanging at the waist from a belt.*
[2] *Same is the skin of ray fish.*

CONCH HORN

Horns made from large conch shells were used during battle. They were covered with a web of knotted threads and had a kumihimo carrying cord.

COMMANDERS BATON

Fans and batons were introduced when the need arose for tactical army manoeuvres. They were used by high ranking Samurai for directing and signalling orders. When they were not in use, they hung by their silk cord from the ring on the front of the armour.

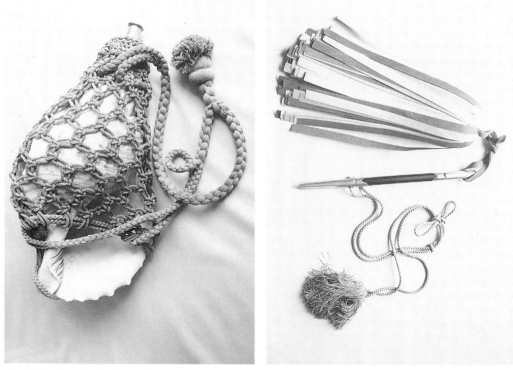

PLATE 29 : (left) Conch shell horn with kumihimo cord.
PLATE 30 :(right) Commander's Baton *(Sai hai)* with a tassel of paper strips
　　　　　　　　and a kumihimo cord.

Courtesy of the Anderson Collection.

CONSTRUCTION

FABRIC

Fabric was a fundamental feature of Samurai Armour. It also provided an opportunity to display rank and status.

Richly decorated silk brocades were very popular especially when Mon or other significant motifs were woven into the design.

Less showy but more practical was a fabric called Asa. It was a common and durable material made from grass-bast fibres such as hemp and ramie.

It could be treated with Shibu *(unripe persimmon juice)* which acted as a waterproofing agent and an insecticide.

Other vegetable fibre fabrics were also used. These included fabrics made from the fibres of wisteria bark *(fuji)* and mulberry *(kozo)*

The influx of foreign goods in the late 16th century, saw the introduction of new fabrics. Indian printed cottons and silks found their way on to armour.

Dutch and English close woven wool became particularly popular with the military, especially for the Kikko brigandine *(see page 55)*.

Armour parts such as sleeves, thigh guards and shin guards were constructed with layers of fabric forming the base.

These layers of fabric were called Iyeji *("foundations of a house")* . Chainmail, metal plates or scales were then sewn onto these shaped areas of fabric to provide the necessary protection.

The 'Iyeji' usually consisted of an underside of plain silk or other fabric, with a showy brocade on the exposed side. Between them lay a courser fabric such as Asa.

The layers were secured with a rice paste glue, before the edges were bound together with a leather or braid trim known as 'Sasheri' *(see page 48)*

(For fabric see plate 33 and 34)

LEATHER

In spite of the Buddhist belief that one should not handle anything from dead animals, leather was an important part of the Samurai's armour.

The preparation of the rawhide was done by the Eta class *(the lowest class)*.

No doubt the processing transformed it into an acceptable item to a devout Buddhist.

The leather was softened by repeatedly bleaching in water and drying in the sun.

It was then printed or smoked *(Kusube)* with a design.

Stencils were made from paper *(Washi)* waterproofed with a coating of Persimmon juice. They were cured and smoked to strengthen them.

Patterns made with small motifs were known as komon. They were frequently used on armour, as they could be shaped to fit into the leather areas.

Shobu Gawa was one of the most popular komon found on armour. The white motif on indigo background represented an Iris plant, presumably chosen because of the 'sword like' leaves. The word Shobu is also a pun on Sho-bu meaning 'correct Samurai' or 'victorious warrior'.

The design evolved over the centuries from a naturalistic form to an increasingly abstract one, culminating with a row of truncating triangles.*(See Diagram 10)*.

Other designs that were used exclusively for armour include ones containing dates written in Chinese characters, such as Tempio Gawa *(733 AD leather)* and Shohei Gawa *(1352 AD leather)*.

These do not represent the date of manufacture, as the designs were reproduced up until the Edo Period. The date is a reference to the year in which they were licensed.*(See plate 35)*.

Other motifs that frequently occur include Chinese lions *(representing courage and ferocity)*, Dragonflies *(favoured by the Samurai because they never go backwards)* and Dragons *(denoting strength)*

LACQUER

The time consuming process of lacquering was highly valued for its ability to preserve things in the humid climate. It has been used in Japan from as early as 500 BC.

Lacquer was made from the sap of a small tree "Rhus Vernicifera". The best quality coming from cuts in the trunk, poorer quality from the branches and twigs.

The sap was heated to remove water, then mixed with various pigments to give it different colours and textures.

Sometimes gold and silver dust was added to give a luxurious finish, though the later has a tendency to tarnish.

DIAGRAM 10 : Various forms of 'Shobu Gawa'.

PAPER

In Japan, paper and textiles are closely linked. Two types of paper fabric, Kamiko and Shifu, were used by the Samurai.

Both used fibres from the bark of Kozo *(a variety of the mulberry tree).*

The dark, outer bark was scrapped away, leaving the pale, inner bark. This was then used to make the paper *(Washi).*

Kamiko was made from a paper with a hatched fibre grain. It was strengthened with coatings of Shibu *(the juice of unripe persimmon fruit)* or Konnyaku Nori *(a solution made from the root of the Konnyaku tuber).*

The sheets of paper were rubbed and crinkled until they could no longer absorb the liquid. The resultant paper, called Momigami *('Rubbed crinkled paper")* , was soft and strong. It was made into a whole variety of garments by glueing and stitching pieces together.

The use of Kamiko appears to date from as early as the Heian period.

It was particularly favoured by the Buddhists, due to its non-animal origins and its association with purity and simplicity.

These qualities also made it popular with the Samurai, particularly during the Kamakura period. To cater for the nobility's desire to display rank, Kamiko was dyed and stencilled in the same manner as textile fabrics. *(Example shown in plate 31 is Shibori, a traditional resist dyeing technique.)*

Shifu *(woven paper cloth)* was derived from the same Kozo fibres, though the paper was made so that the fibres were lying parallel. The paper was sliced into thin strips, then dampened, rolled and spun. It could then be dyed and woven in the same manner as other yarns.

Shifu appears to be a later development evolving from the combined techniques of paper making and weaving of Asa.

It is said that a Samurai of the early 16th century devised a method for making cords of twisted paper which were used as armour lacing. Later they were used as a stronger alternative to straw in the manufacture of sandals.

Wherever the origins of Shifu came from, it was adopted by the Samurai class in both their armour and civilian wear.

PLATE 31 : (top) (from left to right) Kozo bark, Monigami, paper prepared for dyeing and finished Shibori-dyed Kamiko.
PLATE 32 : (bottom) (From left to right) Shifu, Washi and spun paper threads.

Courtesy of Cas Holmes.

EDGE BRAID

All fabric areas in armour are trimmed with either a leather or braid edge known as Sasaheri. The braid most commonly used was of plain weave structure with extra floating threads arranged in rows. These produced a standard ridge pattern.

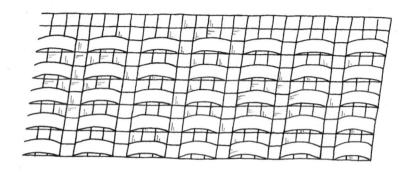

DIAGRAM 11 : Weave of Sasheri braid.

PIPED EDGES

Jabara (*serpent's belly*) is the name given to the decorative piped edge found on armour.

It was made using threads spun from different coloured ply.

Two of these threads, one with an 'S' spin, the other with a 'Z' spin, were laid side-by-side. This created a herringbone effect which was used to conceal joins throughout suits of armour.

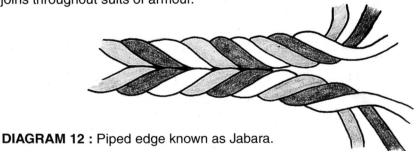

DIAGRAM 12 : Piped edge known as Jabara.

PLATE 33 :(top) Silk brocade with crane motif. Used for outer fabric sections
of armour.

PLATE 34 :(bottom) Fabric used in armour, (left to right) Kusuri dyed cotton,
Asa and indigo dyed crepe silk.

Courtesy of Cas Holmes.

PLATE 35 : Stencilled leather with dates, Chinese lions and peonies.
Courtesy of the Anderson Collection.

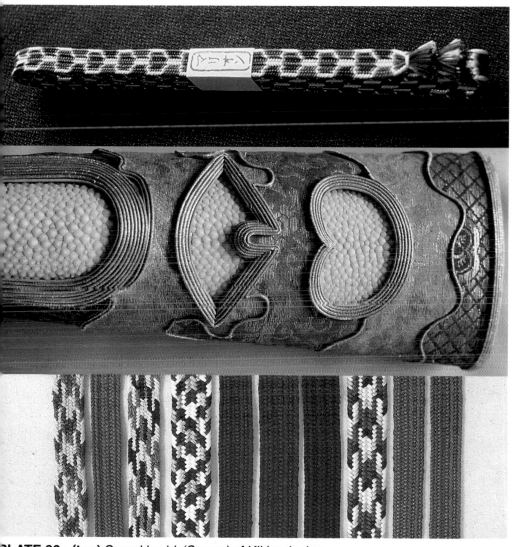

PLATE 36 : (top) Sword braid *(Sageo)* of Kikko design.

Courtesy of Marion Edwards.

PLATE 37 :(middle) Ray skin *(Same)* wrapped in brocade for presentation.
It was used on sword hilts.

Courtesy of the Anderson Collection.

PLATE 38 :(bottom) Modern armour braids, used for Mimi-ito and Odoshi. They
are flat, 8-ridge, twill braids.

PLATE 39: Detail of Thigh guards *(Haidate)* with poppy edging *(Keshi)*,
and Iyozane scales.

Courtesy of Exeter Royal Albert Memorial Museum

FRILLED EDGES

Influenced by the European collars and ruffs, frilled edges called Keshi *(Poppies)* became a fashionable addition to high class armour. They were usually applied to the ends of sleeves and collars, though they could also be found on shoulder guards and thigh guards.

The frill was composed of folded layers of fabric, usually red and white crepe silk. One edge was secured within the fabric of the item being trimmed. The other edge was secured with stitches of green thread.

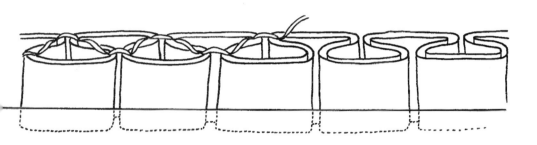

DIAGRAM 13 : Detail of poppy edge*(Keshi)*.

KNOTS

Knots were used as decorative and functional features.

The most predominant knot found on armour is the Agemaki.

It is sometimes known as 'Tombo- Musubi' *(Dragonfly knot)* due to its appearance and the Samurai's fondness for this insect.

The largest and most usual form of the Agemaki can be found at the back of the Do *(Cuirass)*, though smaller, decorative versions can be found in a variety of other places. *(See plate 9)*.

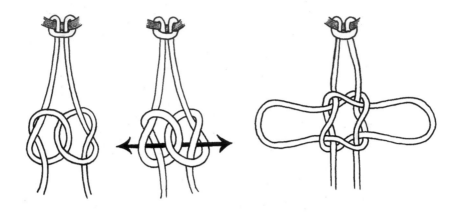

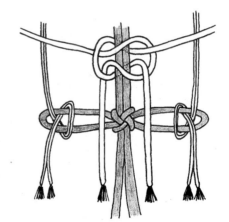

DIAGRAM 14 :(top row)
    How to tie an Agemaki bow.
DIAGRAM 15 :(middle right)
    One way of attaching the
    shoulder guard*(Sode)*
    cords to the Agemaki
    at the back of the cuirass.
DIAGRAM 16 :(bottom right)
    Decorative knot used
    for making loops,
    such as used for Kosaru
    (see diagram 8).

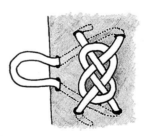

BRIGANDINE

The brigandine known as 'Kikko' *(tortoiseshell)* was a protective area that was both decorative and comfortable.

It was constructed with small hexagonal plates of metal.

These were positioned between layers of fabric. Braid was then laced though the fabric and holes in the plates. This secured the plates in place and formed decorative crosses on the surface of the fabric. Large stitches of thread surrounding the crosses of braid highlighted the hexagonal pattern. *(Kikko can be seen at the top of the Shin guard in plate 13).*

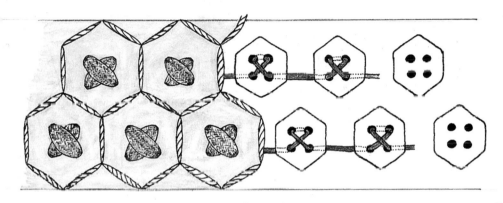

DIAGRAM 17 : Cut away Kikko showing path of the braid.

CHAIN MAIL

The Japanese developed their own unique style chainmail in the Nambokucho period. The mail was usually constructed of metal circles lying flat on the surface with oval links joining them together at right angles. The mail was lacquered and sewn onto fabric backing.

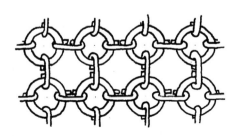

DIAGRAM 18 : One form of Japanese Chainmail.

SCALES AND LACING

SCALES

The scales *(Sane)* used in the lamellar sections of armour were made from either metal or rawhide.

Both types were used together either alternately *(called Ichimai Maze)* or in block areas *(called Kane Maze)*. Suits made entirely of metal scales were much stronger but were rare because they became too heavy to wear.

The rawhide came from cattle or horses and was prepared, stretched and dried before being cut into shape.

Kozane

Scales in the Heian period were large and flat but during the Kamakura period they were reduced in size and built up with lacquer to give them a ribbed shape.

Standard scales known as Kozane were shaped and punched with 13 holes. The 8 lower holes were used for the lower binding and 5 upper holes for the outer lacing.

Shikime zane

Other types of scales were made, such as 'Mizume zane' *(three-eyed scales)* also known as 'Shikime zane' after the style of lacing it was used with *(see page 63)*.

The scale was an elongated version of the Kozane with two columns of holes for overlapping. When laced it produced a triple thickness of scales which strengthened the armour and reduced sagging in the rows.

However, it also made the armour heavy so it was not very popular.

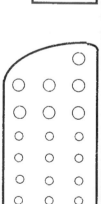

Iyozane

A wide scale called 'Iyozane' was developed in the 14th century.

Only the edges of the scales overlapped. This lessened the number of scales required but caused the rows to weaken. This was remedied by lacing a strip of leather or metal along the back.

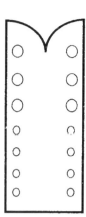

Kiritsuke Kozane

In later years solid plates were used instead of rows of scales.

These cut back on labour as well as increased the strength of the armour.

Some plates were cut and moulded to imitate the original Kozane rows.

These were called 'Kiritsuke Kozane'.

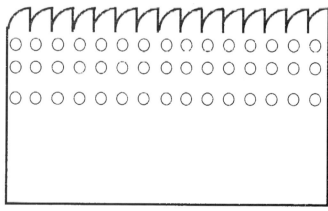

LOWER BINDING

Individual scales were laced in a row with leather thong. This lower binding was known as Shita Toji.

Wild dog skin was said to be preferred because of its low salt content,
thus reducing the risk of rusting.

A special half scale was added on the end of each row to give a uniform thickness along the row.

Originally, each individual scale was lacquered before being bound.

However, economic reasons instigated the lacquering of the whole row after the lower binding *(Shita Toji)* was completed.

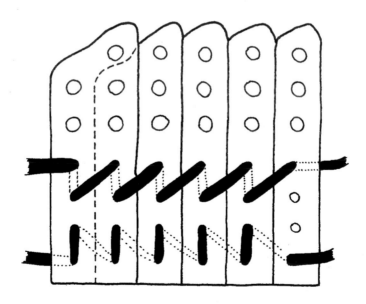

DIAGRAM 19 : One way of making the lower binding *(Shita Toji)*.

EDGE LACE

The completed rows of scales were joined together by a single braid called the Mimi-ito *("ear Thread")*.

Sometimes this braid worked continuously around the whole section but more often it was in three sections. The lowest, horizontal section being called the Uname *(Une= path between rice fields)*

The edge lace *(mimi-ito)* was a stronger and fancier braid than the rest of the lacing. In the Heian period, it was often a design of white with dark blue chevrons, later; light blue was added and the design became known as 'Takanoha Uchi', *(Hawk's feather braid)*.

By the Kamakura and Muromachi period, patterns in white, purple and green or white, red and green were popular.

Navy was added to this combination to give 'Takuboku Uchl' *(woodpecker braid)*. This was a mimi-ito braid of great popularity and was found on most of the later armours. Two reasons for its prominence are given in "Honcho Gunkiko"[1]

The first was that as mimi-ito braids were handed down from father to son, the colours of 'Takuboku' were intended not to clash with any Go-gyo colours.
Go-Gyo were the five elements in which each person's character could be described. Each element was assigned a colour [2] :-

SPRING - EAST- WOOD- BLUE
SUMMER-SOUTH-FIRE-RED
AUTUMN-WEST-METAL-WHITE
WINTER-NORTH-WATER-BLACK
CENTRE-EARTH-YELLOW

---

[1] *Honcho Gunkiko" an important military book written by Arai Hakuseki, in the early 1700's.*
[2] *From Shu-ji (Book of History) dating from around the 6th Century*

The lacing of suits in Go-gyo colours was detailed in Ise Teijo's book "Gun-Yo-KI" after which he suggests one shouldn't take too much notice of it !

The second reason for the popularity of 'Takuboku Uchi', suggested in "Honcho Gunkiko", was that armour laced in just two colours can be called 'Ni-Ke' *(Two colours).*

This was not a good word for a warrior as it is associated with 'Nige' meaning to run away. The addition of the four coloured mimi-ito removed this association.

LACING

The main area of lacing on a suit is referred to as the Odoshi.

The earliest material used for lacing was leather. This could be dyed and patterned.

Though its use was continued throughout the centuries, the preference was for silk braids.

Standard odoshi consisted of flat braids of 8-ridge, twill construction *(see plate 38).*

The braids came in a whole variety of colours, though indigo blue was the most common.

This may have been because indigo dye acted as an ultra-violet filter, thus protecting the silk from light deterioration.

However, red and purple were both popular Samurai colours in spite of the dye rotting the silk.

Madder red was a native dye technique but two new reds, from Safflower and Sappanwood, were introduced from China in the Nara period.

Purple made from the root of the Gromwell plant also arrived at this time.

Colours have long played an important part in emphasising rank and status in the Japanese court, although there were frequent changes in order to accommodate new dyes, techniques and fashions.

This obviously influenced the colour of armour, but ultimately it tended to be a personal choice rather than an indication of rank or family.

Some suits were laced in a combination of plain coloured braids.

The different colours could be used to lace each row in a different shade such as 'Asahi-odoshi' *(dawn lacing)* shading red to pink.

Or the colours could be arranged to form patterns such as seen in the 'Sun and Moon' Sode, *(see plate 10).*

Occasionally the lacing was made with patterned braids, though these were normally reserved for the Edge braid *(mimi-ito).*

In order to thread the braid through the small holes in the scales, the end of the braid was prepared into a needle.

Threads were loosened and trimmed to a tapered point. This was then coated in lacquer to form a hard point which could be used as a needle.

The flexibility of the silk braids enabled wide braids to condense when threaded through the small holes.

When motifs were laced into the armour *(such as in plate 10)* several braids were threaded through a single hole.

PLATE 40 : Making a 'needle' with the end of the braid.

Courtesy of Hiromichi Muira.

Kebiki

With the edge lace *(mimi-ito)* holding the rows in place, the main area of lacing *(Odoshi)* could be filled in. The standard procedure was to lace the rows together horizontally in a style called Kebiki *(Hair Spread over)*.

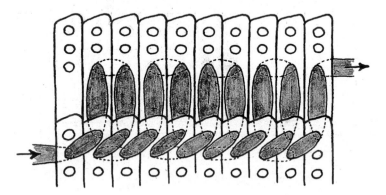

DIAGRAM 20 : Kebiki lacing.

Sugake

A new form of lacing was introduced in the Muromachi era. It was called: 'Ara-Me' *(Rough eye or Sparse point)* though in later years it became known as 'Sugake' *(Simple hang)*.
It required fewer holes in the scales and smaller quantities of braid, resulting in a stronger and more economic armour.

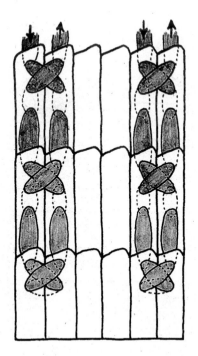

DIAGRAM 21 : Sugake lacing.

Shikime

Another, rarer form of lacing was called
'Shikime me nui' *(cover eye sewing)* ,
sometimes known as 'Chikiri'.
This style of lacing required three sets
of holes so it was used with 'Shikime zane'
(see page 56)

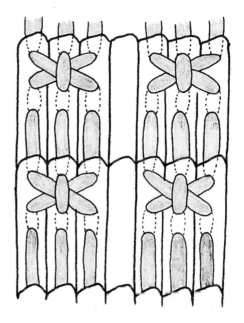

DIAGRAM 22: Shikime lacing.

HISHINUI

The lowest row of scales in a section of armour had the lower binding *(shita toji)*
exposed.
To make this more attractive they were over sewn with red*(madder)* cross knots
known as 'Hishinui'.
An even number of holes in the row were required to give a balanced effect.

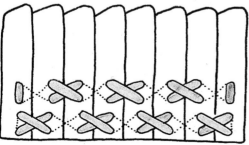

DIAGRAM 23 : Hishinui lacing.

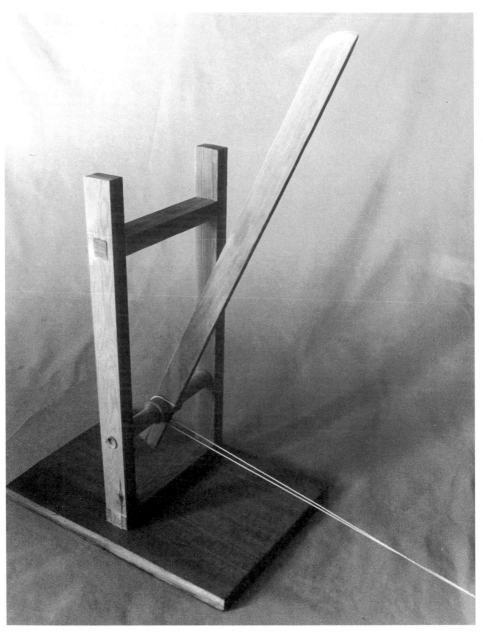

PLATE 41 : Reproduction of a footbeater .
Courtesy of Ernie Henshall.

Kute-Uchi

Research into the antique braids of Japan has usually focused on the beautiful braids associated with the courts and temples.

It has long been thought that braiding equipment was essential to produce these highly complex structures.

However the research of Masako Kinoshita[1] has established that the method referred to as 'Kute-uchi', was the more plausible method for making braids prior to the Edo period.

Kute-uchi *(braiding with hand straps)* is a loop manipulation technique, a method of braiding that can be found throughout the world.

The hand straps were made from lacquered paper rolled over the tops of the loops. These helped to keep the strands in order and protected the lustre of silk being worked.

The earliest existing picture of a braidmaker is on a 15th century scroll " Poetry Match of 71 pairs of Artisans". It clearly shows the loop manipulation technique being employed.

The only equipment shown is a foot operated beater which helps to tighten the stitch being made. This was known as a heshiki *(presser wood)*.

This image of a braidmaker at work is repeated in similar illustrations found in other Japanese documents. *(See plate 44).*

Written text on this form of braiding is almost non existent. The reason for this can be explained by a comment in "Soshun Biko".[2] It compares Kute-uchi with the stand and bobbin method *(see Marudai, page 74).*

It concludes that Kute-uchi is simpler and much quicker, therefore it should be kept confidential.

This was heeded as the following technical instructions were cryptic and incomplete.

---

[1] *Masako Kinoshita is a Japanese/American researcher and author.*
[2] *"Soshun Biko" is part of an unpublished manuscript "Shika Suyo"
(The Thesaurus for Ceasing War) written by Masunari Ozeki in around 1810*

Masako Kinoshita's work in decoding these instructions into practical solutions resulted in braids commonly found on suits of armour.

When one considers the vast quantity of braids used in just one suit and the enormous market for armour, it would seem obvious that a quick, simple method of production would be necessary.

Further evidence that early braids were made using Kute-uchi comes from their structural properties.

Loop manipulation lends itself to the construction of flat braids using an odd number of loops. This results in an element[3] count of an odd number x 2.

Whereas braids of similar appearance made on a Takadai *(see page 77)* have an element count of just an odd number. Marudai braids work with element counts of multiples of 4.

Analysis of pre-Edo braids provided overwhelming evidence in favour of loop manipulation.

Mistakes found in braid work provide another source of structural evidence.

Certain types of mistakes are inherent to the Kute-uchi technique. *(See plate 42)* Many examples of these can be found in early braids, even in the braids from the Shosoin.

PLATE 42 : Mistake in an Odoshi braid.

Courtesy of Surrey Institute or Art & Design.

3 *Threads working together as a unit.*

The following instructions, decoded from "Soshun Biko" by Masako Kinoshita, are for making an odoshi braid. These flat, 8-ridge, twill braids were commonly used in armour.

The number of elements used in these braids varied; the example shown uses 13 loops giving 26 elements.

1) The loop furthest left on the left hand goes around the outside of the loops to become the loop furthest left on the right hand.

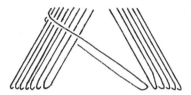

2) The loop furthest right on the right hand goes around the outside of the loops to become the loop furthest on the right on the left hand.

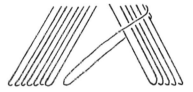

3) The loop furthest left on the left hand goes through the loops and is twisted to become the loop furthest left on the right hand.

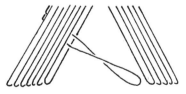

4) The loop furthest right on the right hand goes through the loops to become the loop furthest right on the left hand.

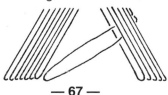

The combined research of Masako Kinoshita and Noemi Speiser
revealed that this Kute-uchi technique could also be applied to the
complex temple braids.
A natural, logical progression from simple braids lead to Kute-uchi; that
could be worked by several braiders interconnecting their loops as they worked.
The resulting complex structures reproduced the famous temple braids with
convincing accuracy.

PLATE 43 : (opposite)

Replicas of historical braids.

They are named after the temple in which they were found.

The replicas were constructed using the Kute-uchi method.

From top to bottom:

1) 72 element braid from Chusonji Temple.(12th century).

2) 132 element braid from Osaka Shitennoji Temple. (12th century).

3) 144 element 'Kikko' braid from Hayatam Taisha.(13th century).

4) Double cloth braid from Hasa Temple. (16th century).

5) 40 element braid from Chion'in Temple. (14th century).

6) Flat braid from Itsukushima Shrine.(12th century)

courtesy of Masako Kinoshita.

Photo by A. Gillis.

PLATE 44 : Print of a Braiders Studio, showing various pieces of equipment.
Courtesy of The Chester Beatty Library, Dublin.

PLATE 45 : Modern necklace inspired by Samurai Armour.
Made from silk Kumihimo braids and porcelain plates.
Courtesy of Linda Caswell.

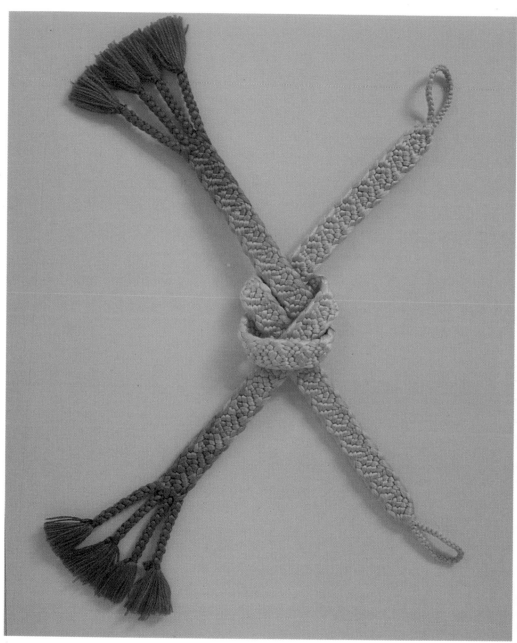

PLATE 46 : Modern Haori Ties.

ABOLITION OF THE SAMURAI

The long line of ruling military Shoguns came to an end with the Meiji Restoration in 1868.
Control of Japan was returned to the Emperor and many changes were instigated.
One, that had a profound effect on the braiding industry was the abolition of the Samurai class.
This, combined with competition from new braiding machines, caused a dramatic decline in the demand for handmade braids.

OBI-JIME

In an effort to maintain a market, a new fashion was introduced.
Wide Obi[1] had been held in place with cloth ties, but they were replaced with Kumihimo braids known as Obi-jime. These braids echoed the Sageo sword braids.

HAORI

Haori jackets were the traditional Japanese half coats. They were originally worn loose, without any ties.
However, Haori braids had been developed from the braids used on tea canisters.
Two short braids, each with a small loop at one end and a tassel at the other, secured the jacket with a choice of knots.
These Obi-jime and Haori ties became the main outlet for kumihimo. They were produced in a whole host of designs to cater for special occasions, status and personal taste.

---

[1] *The material sash of a kimono.*

MODERN KUMIHIMO

There has been a growing preference for Western style clothing in Japan.
As a consequence, the use of kimono with its Obi-jime has declined.
However Kumihimo has survived, mainly due to the establishment of Japanese braiding schools. They offer tuition in the technique that was once a closely guarded secret.
Access to information and materials has enabled the craft to become available to anyone.
This has ensured the survival of the traditional Kumihimo methods and has opened up the possibilities for new discoveries.

A whole variety of equipment has been associated with the production of Kumihimo, although only four pieces are in common use today.
It is hard to establish exactly when each piece was introduced but by the Edo period they were all in existence.

MARUDAI

The Marudai *(Round stand)* is the most common and versatile piece of braiding equipment in use today.
The round top of the stand has a central hole at which all the threads converge.
The threads divide across the top and hang around the circumference.
They are held under tension by weighted, wooden bobbins.
Braids are produced by moving the threads across the surface to new positions.
Different sets of moves produce different structured braids.
The interlacing at the central hole is gradually pulled down by a counterbalance weight attached underneath.

PLATE 47 : Kumihimo being worked on a Marudai.

KAKUDAI

The Kakudai *(Square stand)* functions much the same as a Marudai.

The main difference being that the counterbalance draws the braid upwards instead of down. This means that the braider is working around the exterior rather than the interior of the braid.

The stand is square and often has fabric wrapped around the legs. This is to prevent the bobbins from unspinning when twist has been added to the threads.

The braids produced on a Kakudai are similar to Marudai braids although the Kakudai specialises in twisted ones.

AYATAKEDAI

An Ayatakedai *(Bamboo Stand)* is a loom-like structure which produces flat braids with a warp and weft structure.

There are bamboo slats along one edge of the stand. The warp threads are positioned on notches along these slats.

The threads are attached to weighted bobbins and are moved to produce different weaving stitches. The weft threads are attached to bobbins that hang at right-angles to the warp.

The stitches made by the warp threads are secured by crossing the weft threads between them.

The stitches are beaten into place by a bamboo 'Hera' *("sword" or "spatula")*

Flat braids with textured weave are a characteristic of Ayatakedai work.

TAKADAI

The Takadai *(High Stand)* is a large piece of wooden equipment with two rows of runners on each side. Wooden pegs are set into sliding blocks which move along these runners. The pegs separate the threads which are wound onto weighted bobbins.

Braids are constructed by taking the furthest most bobbin on one side, passing it through the threads and repositioning it on the opposite side. This creates an oblique weave where the warp and weft threads are interchangeable. The stitches are also beaten with a 'Hera'.

The Takadai produces flat, single or double cloth braids. Braids with elaborate woven motifs are a distinctive feature of Takadai work

PLATE 48 : Takadai *(High Stand).*

Bibliography

Adachi, Fumie, *"Japanese Design Motifs"* Dover, USA, 1972.
Allen, Jeanne, *"The Designer's Guide to Samurai Patterns"* Thames & Hudson, UK,1990.
Anderson, L.J, *"Japanese Armour"* UK 1968.
Bottomley, Ian & Hopson,Anthony,*"Arms and Armour of the Samurai"* Crescent, USA, 1990.
Carey, Jacqui *"Kumihimo"* article in 'Text' UK. 1994.
Harano, Mitsuko (editor) *"Kumihimo"* Hoikusha, Japan, 1977.
Harris, Jennifer (editor) *"5000 years of Textiles"* British Museum Press, U.K. 1993.
Holmes, Cas, *"Japan's Ancient Skill of Papermaking"*, unpublished Winston Churchill
                            Memorial Fellowship study report, 1985.
Kinoshita, Masako *"Study of Archaic Braiding Techniques in Japan"* Kyoto Shoin, 1994.
Kinoshita, Masako *"A Braiding Technique Documented in an early C19th Japanese Treatise
          'Soshun Biko'"* article in 'The Textile Museum Journal ', USA.1986.
Kinoshita, Masako *" The Traditional Silk Braids of Japan"* article in 'Piecework' USA. 1995.
Kinoshita, Masako *"Kute-Uchi: A Pre-Edo technique of making lacing and other braids for
          Japanese armour "* article in Journal of the International Association
                            of Costume,1994.
Martin, Catherine, *"Kumihimo"* Old Hall Press,UK,1986.
Martin, Catherine, *"Kumihimo: The Japanese Art of Braid Making"* article in 'Crafts' UK. 1984.
Minnich, Helen, *"Japanese Costume"* Charles Tuttle Co. Japan, 1963.
Office of Shosoin,*"Shosoin no Kumihimo"*, Heibonsha,Japan, 1973.
Ohamaguchi, San & Talbot, Clifton *" Fortune Telling by Japanese Swords"*
                            John Lane, UK,1905.
Owen, Rodrick, *"The Big Book of Sling and Rope Braids"*, Cassell, UK, 1995.
Rathbun, William, *"Beyond the Tanabata Bridge"* Thames and Hudson, UK, 1993.
Robert, L.P. *"Robert's Guide to Japanese Museums"* Kodansha, Japan.
Tokoro, Hoko, *"Kumihimo in Japan"*, Ogaki Unesco Association, Japan, 1983.
Robinson, H. Russell (editor)*"The Manufacture of Armour and Helmets in 16th Century
                            Japan* 'Holland Press, UK, 1962.
Robinson, H. Russell (editor)*"The Armour Book in Honcho Gunkiko"* Holland Press, UK 1964
Turnbull, Stephen, *"The Book of the Samurai"* Arms & Armour Press, UK, 1982.
Sahashi, Kei (editor) *"Exquisite: The World of Japanese Kumihimo Braiding"* Kodansha,
                            Japan,1988.
Speiser, Noemi *"The Manual of Braiding"* Speiser,Switzerland 1983.
Speiser, Noemi *"The Art of Japanese Braiding"* article in CIBA Geigy Review, Switzerland,
                            1974.
Sugimura, Tsune, *"The Enduring Crafts of Japan"* Walker & Weatherhill, Japan.
Tada, Makiko, *"Kumihimo"* Japanese Festival Office, UK 1984.
Yang, Sunny & Narasin, Rochelle, *"Textile Art of Japan"* Shufunotomo, Japan.

INDEX